Black Love Notes to Self

MELISSA A. MITCHELL

MYND MATTERS

Published by Mynd Matters Publishing
715 Peachtree Street NE
Suites 100 & 200
Atlanta, GA 30308
www.myndmatterspublishing.com

978-1-957092-63-8 (pbk)
978-1-957092-64-5 (hdcv)

SECOND EDITION

As colorful as life is, sometimes it really is just black and white.

It is, or it isn't.
It's yours, or it's not.
It's right, or it's wrong.

You will face many crossroads that will require you to make a choice. Whatever direction you head in, know that you hold the compass that leads you to your destiny.

This book urges you to think inside the box. The black squares represent sitting inside your own brilliant mind to find all the answers that you need.

I dedicate this collection of precious mantras to those who help keep the world spinning on its axis by simply being themselves. My dad used to say, "Being who you are is always in style, and all the other personalities are taken anyway."

Knowing who you are and whose you are is key to every level of success you aspire to achieve. May you find a few gems between these pages that will propel you on your golden journey to the greatest version of yourself.

A DREAMER needs a PLANNER.

Allowing yourself to be loved while you're healing is a superpower.

SOMETIMES IT'S NOT ABOUT
TRUSTING GOD. IT'S ABOUT
TRUSTING YOURSELF ENOUGH
TO SEE IT THROUGH.

AGE AIN'T NOTHING BUT AN ILLUSION.

An **OVERTHINKER** needs a **LISTENER.**

Always go into a relationship with the thought that what you give is more important than what you can get.

Keep your eyes on God and everything else will fall into place.

capture and savor every moment. soon they will be memories.

Don't be in such a rush to get to the next part.

even with all the amazing things that have happened in your life thus far, God still has more in store for you.

If it doesn't make you feel good, stop.

If you did it out of love, there are no losses.

Applaud
yourself
for the small
wins too.
By the time big
ones come,
you will be used to
celebrating yourself.

Consistency is key...
but so is being a good person.

Be careful what you speak
out of your mouth. Your words
can build a house you don't want
to live in and create a path you
don't want to walk on.

yes, sending memes all day is a love language.

Don't talk yourself out of answered prayers.

PREPARE FOR EVERYTHING YOU'RE ASKING GOD FOR.

Be very clear about what you want.

It's never luck. It's always God.

Be wise with your use of time and talents. Everybody and everything doesn't deserve you.

Don't let social media make you jealous of what you should be inspired by.

BY THE TIME
THEY REALIZE
YOUR WORTH,
YOU WILL BE
WORTH SO
MUCH MORE.

Everything about you should reflect what you're praying for.

Chile, get your
rest before your
body chooses
to rest for you.

GOD STILL HAS PLENTY OF TIME TO DO WHAT HE SAID HE WOULD DO FOR ME THIS YEAR.

MAKE SURE YOU LEAVE A ROOM BETTER THAN HOW YOU FOUND IT.

Happiness is an inside job and a full-time job.

Don't envy a
life that you know
nothing about.
Everyone has a
journey to
their promise.
Be committed
to your own.

DON'T EVER THINK SMILES COME WITHOUT A COST.

God will let the
system glitch
just for you.

Don't stay too low, too long.

God, I'm thanking you as if it has already happened.

Don't talk
yourself
out of
what you
know you
deserve.

Feel your feelings. All of them.

I DON'T HAVE ALL THE ANSWERS, BUT I STAY CONNECTED TO WHO DOES.

EVERY year is my year.

If they really wanted to, they would have.

How bad do you want it?

EVERYTHING YOU ARE IS EVERYTHING SOMEONE IS SPECIFICALLY LOOKING FOR.

FAITH IS SEEING IT THROUGH REGARDLESS OF HOW IT LOOKS.

I'm always going to be taken care of because I really live out the quotes I post.

If you haven't searched for the answer yet, please don't ask me.

God is ready to show you
how good it gets!
Are you ready?
Can you handle it?
Do you have a plan?

IF YOU DON'T
BELIEVE YOU
DESERVE
SOMETHING,
HOW DO
YOU THINK
YOU WILL
ACTUALLY
MANIFEST IT?

How can you ask for increase when you never finish what you start?

God will break the rules to bless me.

Eventually you will get everything you prayed for... with upgrades.

Don't underestimate the power of showing up.

IT ALL WORKS OUT. ALL OF IT.

I want a lot. So I pray a lot, work a lot, do a lot, and expect a lot.

LOVE IS A PRIVILEGE AND AN ASSIGNMENT. DON'T TAKE IT LIGHTLY.

I don't
make the
rules,
I'm just the
exception
to them.

I'd rather wait for a God win.

God put it on you because it is you. You're the answer.

I'M NOT MEAN.
I JUST MEAN
WHAT I SAY.

GO EASY ON YOURSELF.
GOD ISN'T FOCUSED ON
HOW MUCH YOU HAVEN'T
DONE. HE'S PROUD OF
YOUR EFFORT AND
INTENTION FOR WHAT YOU
HAVE DONE. BE LIKE GOD.

*If we can't laugh and cry together,
how can we build together?*

Instead of praying for more, ask for better management of what you have.

If you ever had
a chance to
experience real
love, you know
God is real.

IMAGINE BEING TOO AFRAID TO FOLLOW YOUR DREAMS, AND YOU MISS OUT ON THE LIFE GOD REALLY WANTED FOR YOU.

If you're praying for a different life, be prepared to do life differently.

ISOLATION IS ONE OF GOD'S GREATEST CLASSROOMS.

Just try.
Stop
just
dreaming.

IF YOU'RE REALLY EXPECTING SOMETHING (TO HAPPEN), YOU SHOULD VIGOROUSLY PREPARE FOR IT. MAKE SPACE FOR YOUR NEXT YES.

Keep dreaming big,
God will send the
help you need.

Never stop believing that it could happen for you.

MAY GOD GRANT YOUR DEEPEST DESIRES, ANSWER YOUR BIGGEST PRAYERS, AND USHER IN YOUR GRANDEST IDEAS.

If it's for you, it won't be tangled in confusion. That's how you know it's from God.

It takes great strength to show your weaknesses.

It's not always about talent but it's always about energy.

IT'S OKAY TO BUILD A TEAM.

You are building your legacy with what you do daily.

Just know God doesn't play about you.

op waiting for the perfect moment for anything. Do it now, do it all, and do it now all the time.

Loving yourself looks like taking a moment to enjoy everything you've worked so hard to have.

Nothing you have done for God has gone unnoticed.

One idea can lead to one million. Trust your imagination.

SMILE AS IF EVERYONE IS WATCHING.

Soak up images of things you want to manifest before you go to sleep so they will slip into your subconscious.

w requires overtime. Are you ready to change your habits to manage your manifestations?

MY LOVE LANGUAGE
IS REMINDING PEOPLE
I LOVE TO PURSUE
THE DREAMS THEY
WHISPERED TO ME
IN FAITH.

optimism is a choice.

someone else winning doesn't mean you can't win too.

SPEND YOUR MONEY AND YOUR TIME WISELY.

Sometimes silence is **LOUD.**

Speaking life into the right man can change the world.

ONE CAN
LITERALLY COME
INTO YOUR LIFE AND
MAKE EVERYTHING
THAT FAILED BEFORE
THEM MAKE SENSE.

Someone is always watching.

Purpose is what keeps you on Earth and opens doors for you that you never imagined.

Some of your best creations show up when you don't feel like it.

O MANY BLESSINGS ARE FOUND IN THAT LAST BIT OF ENERGY YOU'RE ABLE TO EXERT. IT IS IN THAT MOMENT WHERE GOD SHOWS UP TO GET YOU TO THE FINISH L I N E .

Sometimes

the

only

way

out

is

in.

Stop allowing what has happened to impact what will happen.

TAKE PICTURES. LOTS OF THEM.

Stop letting the world taint your trust in God.

THE LOVE WILL COME.
THE CALLS WILL COME.
THE PEACE WILL COME.
THE MONEY WILL COME.
THE OPPORTUNITIES WILL COME.
YOU WILL NOT MISS ANYTHING
THAT BELONGS TO YOU.

Watching my silent prayers become my public reality is my favorite genre.

Stop asking people to do stuff for free. You have no idea how much it costs to be them...*and I'm not just talking about money.*

The rules are fake.
Just live, Baby!

sometimes you don't have energy for nothing and nobody. And that's okay.

What I do doesn't have to make sense to you because you didn't hear what God told me.

The best revenge is doing everything you said you would, when they really thought you couldn't.

Stop begging to be included, only for you not to show up with the right energy.

There's more than enough for everyone. God won't run out.

The reality is, you are living out the consequences of your bravery. If you don't like your experiences, be brave enough to pray higher prayers.

The heirs to my father's throne are counting on me to make the right decision in love and in life.

WHILE YOU'RE WAITING FOR WHATEVER—STILL ENJOY THE DAYDREAMS, AND VISIONS, AND THE RANDOM THOUGHTS. THEY ALL KEEP YOU WHIMSICAL.

Stop letting your actions contradict your prayers.

There is too much information out here to still make uninformed decisions.

STOP
DOUBTING
YOUR
ANSWERED
PRAYERS
IN
HUMAN
FORM.

They can't see your vision because
God didn't give it to them.
God gave it to you.
Trust that and stay focused.

Trust God so much
that people think
you look crazy. That
means you're dreaming
big enough.

A VISIONARY SEES A CLOSED DOOR AS A WELCOMED CHALLENGE. THEY REALIZE YOU JUST NEED TO TURN THE KNOB, INSTEAD OF IT BEING WIDE OPEN.

When in doubt, ask yourself: is this really God's BEST for me?

Those quiet tears and struggles will have a loud and public victory. Don't be afraid to praise God out in the open.

WHEN GOD IS TRULY YOUR SOURCE, YOU WILL NEVER RUN OUT OF IDEAS.

An unanswered prayer is not an unheard one.

THE
RIGHT
PERSON
SEES
YOUR
CONSISTENCY.

Stop being so hard on yourself. You're closer than you think.

THE WEIGHT OF BEING AN ENTREPRENEUR AND VISIONARY IS HEAVY.

THE WORK NO ONE SEES WILL SOON BE REWARDED.

What God is about to do for me doesn't have to make sense to anyone... including me.

There's no extra credit in Heaven for overworking yourself.

Yes, it's too good to be true. But yes, God is doing it just for you.

To be loved by an artist is a magical experience.

You
have
more
in you
than
you think
you do.

THE BEST WAY TO PREDICT THE FUTURE IS TO CREATE IT.

YES, I KNOW THERE IS A TIMELINE AND PROCESS FOR SOME LEVELS OF SUCCESS, BUT I ALSO KNOW THAT ONE YES FROM GOD WILL MAKE UP FOR ALL LOST TIME.

Don't let
what you see
impact what
you know to
be true.

you can be your own inspiration.

WHEN YOU GIVE A WOMAN WITH VISION AN IDEA, IT WILL BECOME AN EMPIRE.

MONEY IS GOD'S IDEA. WEALTH IS GOD'S DESIRE. ABUNDANCE IS GOD'S PROMISE.

Stop lowering your standards to fit in with people. You are who you are for a reason.

God can change your circumstances for the better at any moment.

Life goes on after loss
but stop to remember
what a gift it is to be
reading this message.

I'M NOT IN AN OPEN RELATIONSHIP – I'M OPEN TO WHATEVER GOD ALLOWS IN THIS RELATIONSHIP.

Yes, I'm too good for certain things because at one point I settled for too long.

May we have the courage to trade in a paycheck for an empire.

PASSION

is

a

hell

of

a

drug.

Be grateful for inclusion. But survive without it.

YOU CAN NEVER

GIVE MORE THAN

GOD CAN REPLACE.

You can't tell God how to answer your prayers.

YOU HAVE NO
IDEA WHAT PEOPLE
BATTLE EACH DAY
AND YOU DON'T
NEED TO. BE GENTLE
WITH PEOPLE.

Many people haven't made it to the next level because they are afraid. The next level can sense your fear and won't show up until you're ready.

You
just can't
do regular
living.
Do it grand
every day.

Do the work that will usher your answered prayers.

THEY DON'T HAVE TO
SEE WHAT YOU SEE
WHEN YOU SEE IT.
TRUST YOUR GUT BUT
MOST IMPORTANTLY,
TRUST YOUR GOD.

You have to hold on to your faith even when nothing seems to be happening. In a moment, God can give you all the time back you think you've wasted.

CONSIDER THE SOURCE WHEN TAKING ADVICE. NOT EVERYONE IS EQUIPPED TO PROVIDE KEEN WISDOM. THE SAFEST BET IS TO SEEK THE ULTIMATE SOURCE. IF YOU FIND DIFFICULTY HEARING HIS VOICE, DELVE INTO HIS WORD.

you

never

know

who

you

are

influencing.

The enemy fears your future so he tries to keep you oppressed and depressed. You have to press on to your promised big finish. You have it in you!

YOU'RE WAITING ON GOD AND THE WHOLE TIME HE'S BEEN WAITING ON YOU.

Where you are isn't your destination but part of your journey.

Stop waiting until a special occasion to celebrate how far you've come. Making it to today is an accomplishment on its own.

You will get everything accomplished that God has assigned to your name. Stop looking at the clock and the calendar. God will make it happen.

Wait for something (and someone) that is soul stirring. You will know it once you experience it. Nothing is greater than finding that "thing" that makes you disregard space and time.

YOU CAN'T OUTTHINK GOD SO STOP TRYING TO. USE YOUR ENERGY ELSEWHERE.

Choosing me will always be worth the sacrifice.

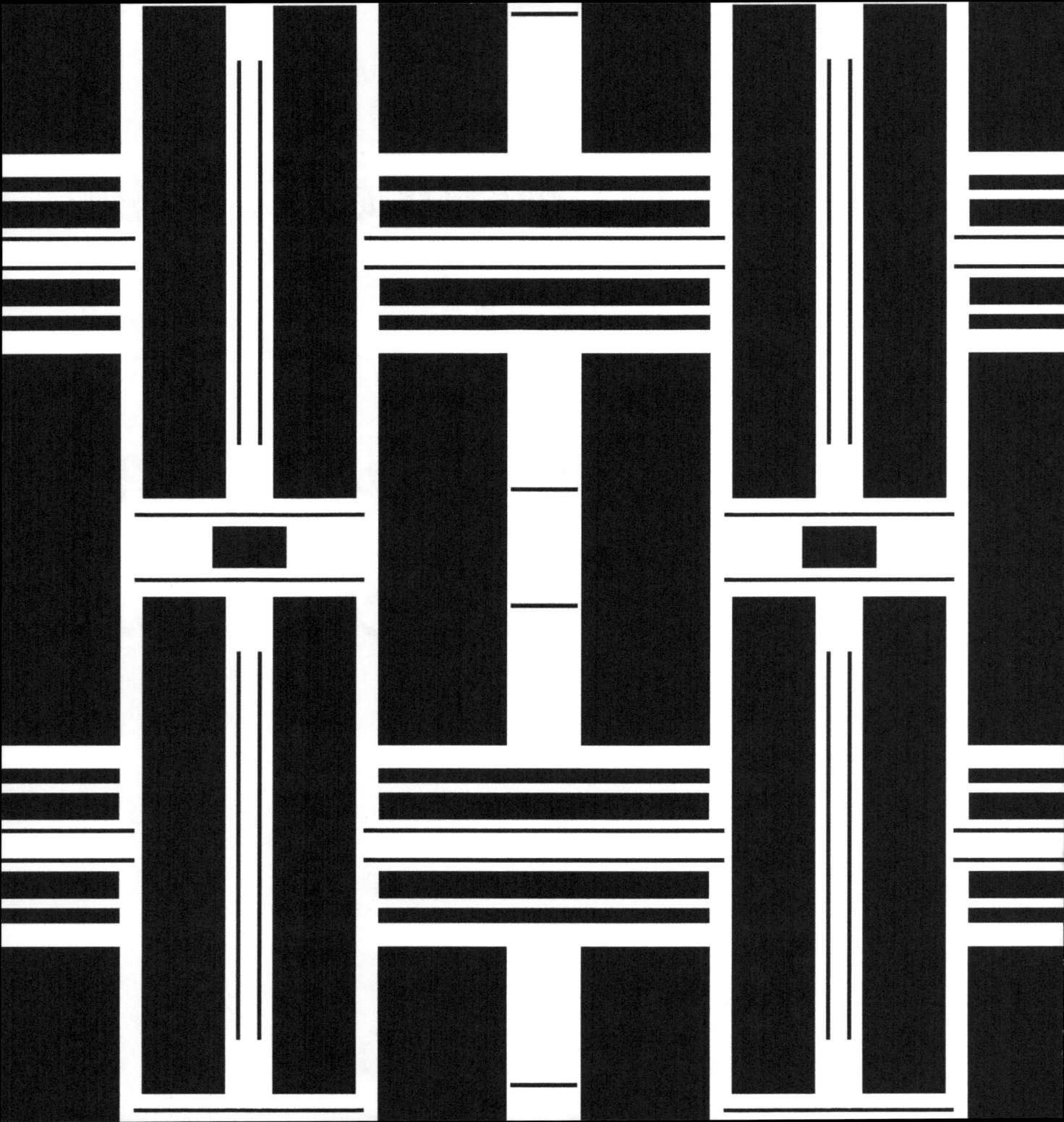

ONE YES FROM GOD WILL MAKE UP FOR ANY "LOST" TIME.

God has the answer before you even have the question.

Someone else winning doesn't mean you can't win, too.

Make sure you
leave a room
better than how
you found it.

STOP SETTLING WHEN YOU KNOW MORE IS POSSIBLE FOR YOU.

Just when you think there are no more options, here comes God with yet another miracle for you.

For the record, 99.9% of the messages a motivator shares are merely words they've once spoken to themselves.

YOUR THOUGHTS ESTABLISH YOUR CIRCUMSTANCES. ALIGN YOUR THINKING WITH HIS WORD AND WATCH HIM MOVE LIKE NEVER BEFORE.

It's amazing how encouraging others actually encourages yourself.

OD OPERATES ABOVE OUR THINKING. HE PLANS TO BLESS US BEYOND OUR WILDEST DREAMS. SO DREAM WITHOUT MEASURE!

You only need one person to believe IN you, to believe FOR you, and believe **THROUGH** you.

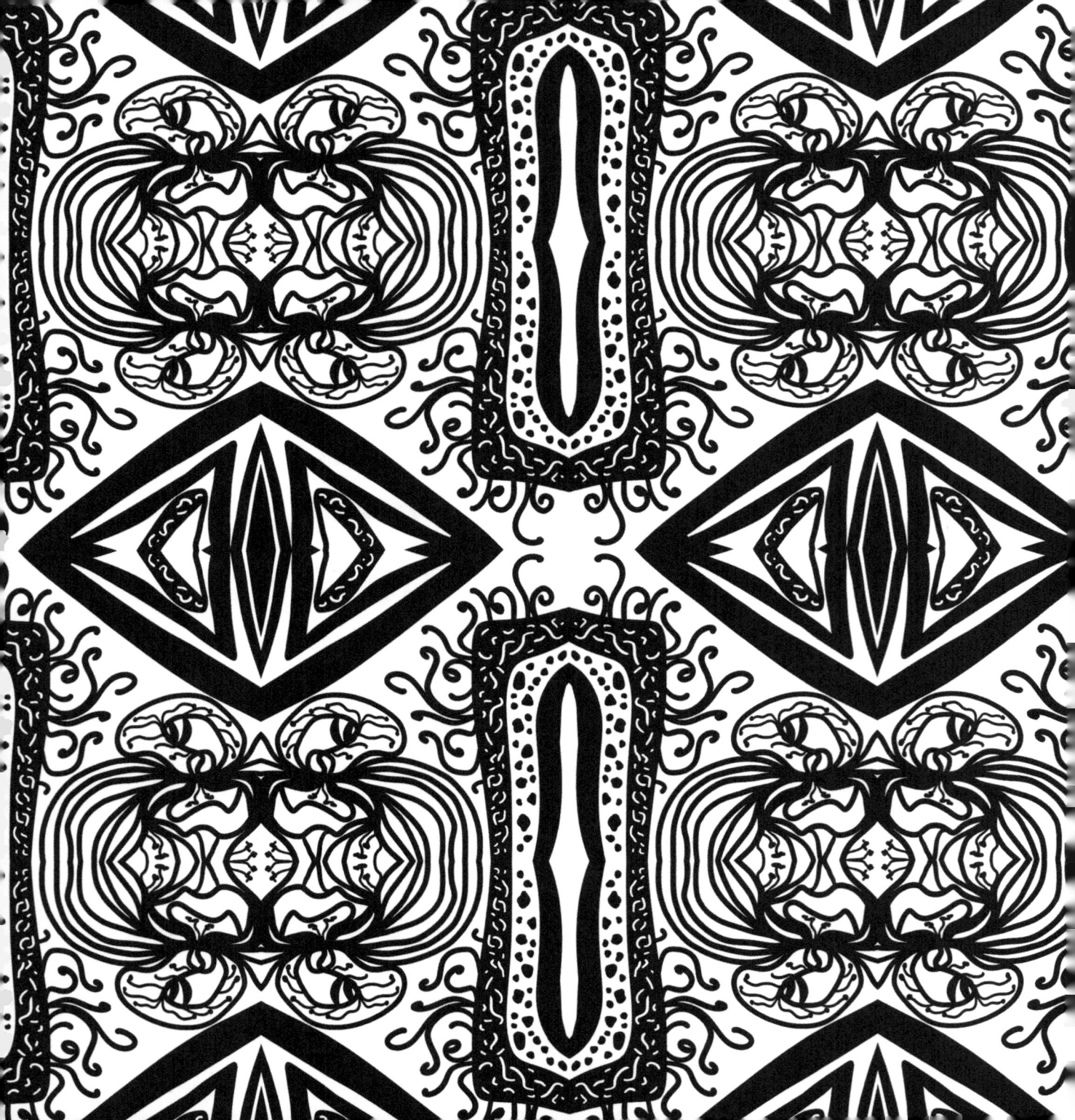

Time alone allows
you to learn things
that are difficult
to learn while
with someone.
Don't resent your
isolation because
it's valuable time
to learn who you
really are.

God likes to hear what you will do when it happens. But he loves to see what you are willing to do with what you have now.

THERE IS NO
NEED TO EXPLAIN
WHAT GOD ONLY
SPOKE TO YOU.
IF HE WANTED
OTHERS TO KNOW,
HE WOULD HAVE
TOLD THEM. TRUST
GOD'S WORDS
FOR YOU.

Learn to dream beyond your comfort zone.

THANK GOD IN ADVANCE FOR BLESSINGS YOU NEVER SAW COMING.

When the right love flows through your life, it feels like the perfect remedy to an unknown ailment.

For someone, you are an answered prayer.